Language Arts Tutor: Grammar

By
CINDY BARDEN

COPYRIGHT © 2005 Mark Twain Media, Inc.

ISBN   10-digit: 1-58037-286-4
        13-digit: 978-1-58037-286-2

Printing No. CD-404013

Mark Twain Media, Inc., Publishers
Distributed by Carson-Dellosa Publishing LLC

Visit us at www.carsondellosa.com

HPS 231721

Table of Contents

1   Introduction
2   From Aardvarks to Zippers: Nouns
3   Leaves, Potatoes, and Daisies: Singular and Plural Nouns
4   Do Mouses Live in Houses?: Irregular Noun Plurals
5   London Bridge Is Not in England Anymore: Proper Nouns
6   Hop, Skip, and Jump: Action Verbs
7   Strange, But True: Singular and Plural Verbs
8   To Be, or Not To Be: Verbs of Being
9   Past, Present, or Future?: Verb Tense
10 Three Forms of Verbs: Present, Past, and Past Participle
11 Sing, Sang, Sung: Irregular Verbs
12 At the White House: Complete Sentences
13 What's the Question?: Interrogative and Exclamatory Sentences
14 Please Hand Me That Mountain: Declarative and Imperative Sentences
15 Rachel Giggled: Simple Predicates
16 Hey, Diddle, Diddle: Simple Subjects
17 Match-Ups: Agreement of Subjects and Predicates
18 Putting It All Together: Writing Complete Sentences
19 Putting It All Together: Subject/Predicate Word List
20 Getting Personal: Pronouns Are Subjects
21 They're Bringing Their Tubas: Possessive Pronouns
22 Don't Be Confused: Contractions and Possessive Pronouns
23 The Audience Threw Flowers: Direct and Indirect Objects
24 What Fell From the Sky?: Interrogative Pronouns
25 Stinky Cheese on Crisp, Crunchy Crackers: Adjectives
26 Faster Than a Locomotive: Comparative and Superlative Adjectives
27 Long, Longer, Longest, But Never Wrong, Wronger, Wrongest: Comparative and Superlative Adjectives
28 Use Your Senses: Sensory Words
29 On the Way to Denver: Adverbs
30 Soon, Sooner, Soonest: Comparative and Superlative Adverbs
31 Adjective or Adverb?: Adjectives and Adverbs
32 Across the Wide Missouri: Prepositions/Prepositional Phrases
33 When in Rome: Prepositions/Prepositional Phrases
34 She Met Him and Me: Objective Pronouns
35 He Knew the New Gnu: Homophones
36 What's the Connection?: Conjunctions
37 Did He Really Say That?: Identify Parts of Speech
38 Five-Letter Nouns: Noun Word Search
39 Mabel Likes to Polka in Her Polka-dotted Dress: More Than One Part of Speech
40 Parts of Speech Bingo Card
41 Parts of Speech Bingo Word List
43 Answer Keys

Introduction

Students of all ability levels prefer interesting and readable material, particularly those who struggle with grammar in their writing. The Language Arts Tutor series engages the interests of these students through individualized tutoring in highly readable, age-appropriate activities. The series introduces and strengthens the concepts needed to build and reinforce grammar skills for students in grades four through eight.

The Tutor series comprises an array of titles in reading, math, science, and language arts. Designed in a lively, non-intimidating format, the reproducible activities include stories, exercises, games, riddles, puzzles, and other stimulating materials to improve grammatical skills and enrich the learning experience for the struggling learner.

The activities in this book focus on learning to identify the basic parts of speech; matching nouns and pronouns in gender, case, and number; writing positive, comparative, and superlative adjectives and adverbs; and writing complete sentences with subjects and predicates that agree.

A sidebar on each page clearly states the concept or skill reinforced by that activity. This format allows students to master one concept or skill at a time, thereby building confidence and proficiency.

Tutors can meet the special needs of students by selecting specific activities that reinforce the skills each student needs most.

Name: _____ Date: _____

From Aardvarks to Zippers

A **noun** is a word that names a person, place, thing, or idea. *Egg, hiccup, burp, carpenter,* and *love* are nouns.

Directions: Underline the nouns in each sentence.

1. A regulation golf ball has 336 dimples.

2. Sharks are the only fish that can blink with both eyes.

3. In 1927, long-distance telephone service between New York and London cost $75.00 for the first three minutes.

4. Coin-operated pay telephones first appeared in 1899.

5. The yo-yo is not a recent invention: children in ancient Rome played with these toys made of wood or metal over 2,500 years ago.

Directions: For each category, write five nouns.

Plants	Transportation	Occupations
_____	_____	_____
_____	_____	_____
_____	_____	_____
_____	_____	_____
_____	_____	_____

Weather Words	Places	Ideas
_____	_____	_____
_____	_____	_____
_____	_____	_____
_____	_____	_____
_____	_____	_____

Name: _____ Date: _____

Leaves, Potatoes, and Daisies

Nouns can be singular or plural. **Singular** means one. **Plural** means more than one. Most nouns form their plurals by adding an *s* at the end of the word. *Pizzas, lawyers, noodles,* and *garages* are plural nouns.

Words that end in *f, s, o,* and *y* are often exceptions to the rule. When in doubt, check a dictionary.

Antonyms are words that mean the opposite. *Men* and *women; dogs* and *cats;* and *mountains* and *valleys* are antonyms.

Directions: Write the plurals. Use a dictionary to check the spelling.

1. leaf _____
2. fly _____
3. trophy _____
4. elf _____
5. hippopotamus _____
6. sky _____
7. bus _____
8. ox _____
9. address _____
10. box _____

Directions: For each noun, write another noun that is an antonym.

11. water _____
12. questions _____
13. adults _____
14. friends _____
15. days _____
16. ceilings _____
17. aunt _____
18. slavery _____
19. city _____
20. smile _____

Name: _____ Date: _____

Do Mouses Live in Houses?

The **spellings** of some nouns change completely from singular to plural, as in *child - children; mouse - mice.*

Both the singular and plural of some nouns are spelled the same, for example: *cattle - cattle.*

Directions: Write the plurals of these nouns. Use a dictionary if you need help.

	Singular	Plural
1.	man	_____
2.	woman	_____
3.	goose	_____
4.	louse	_____
5.	scissors	_____
6.	sheep	_____
7.	moose	_____
8.	tooth	_____
9.	foot	_____
10.	fish	_____
11.	deer	_____
12.	data	_____
13.	crisis	_____
14.	bacterium	_____
15.	analysis	_____

Name: _____   Date: _____

London Bridge Is Not in England Anymore

A **proper noun** is a noun that names a specific person, place, or thing. *Harry Potter, Mississippi River, Mount Vesuvius,* and *London Bridge* are proper nouns.

London Bridge

Directions: Underline the proper nouns in the following sentences.

1. The 60-foot-high heads of four presidents, George Washington, Thomas Jefferson, Abraham Lincoln, and Theodore Roosevelt, were carved on Mount Rushmore in the Black Hills of South Dakota by Gutzon Borglum.

2. Yellowstone National Park in Wyoming, Montana, and Idaho became the first national park in 1872 by order of President Ulysses S. Grant.

3. Eight states, Maine, Maryland, Massachusetts, Michigan, Minnesota, Mississippi, Missouri, and Montana, begin with *m*.

4. Harriet Tubman, known as the "Moses of her people," led slaves to freedom on the Underground Railroad.

5. We celebrate Thanksgiving on the fourth Thursday in November.

Directions: Use the Internet or other reference sources to find one interesting fact about each topic. Write a sentence about each topic that includes at least four proper nouns.

6. An athlete: _____

_____

7. A city, state, or country: _____

_____

8. A lake, river, or ocean: _____

_____

9. A book, movie, or play: _____

_____

Name: _____ Date: _____

Hop, Skip, and Jump

A **verb** is a word that shows action or being. *Tiptoe, bounce,* and *fly* are action verbs.

Directions: As you hop along the path, write an action verb that begins with the letter on each stepping stone. For *x*, use any verb that contains the letter *x*.

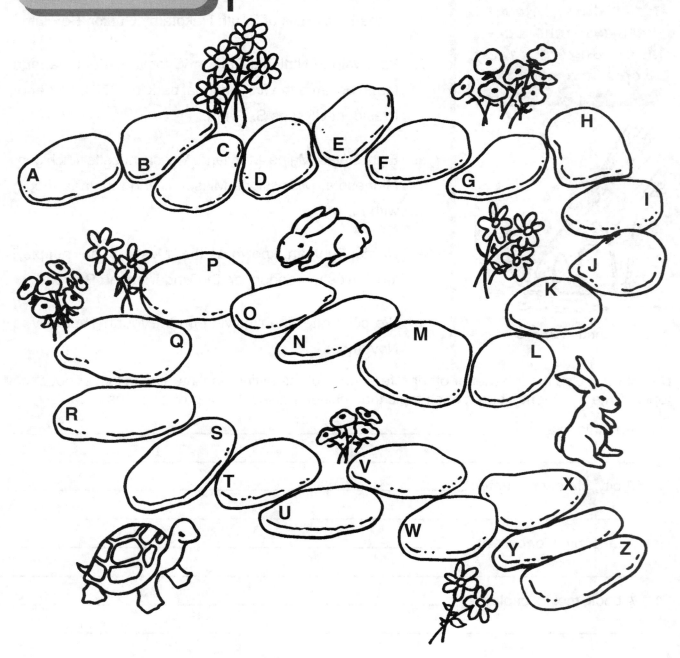

Name: _____   Date: _____

Strange, But True

Nouns that end in an *s* are usually plural. Some examples are: *The boys go; The girls sing; The birds chirp.* **Verbs** that end in *s* are usually singular. Some examples are: *She goes; He sings; It chirps.*

Directions: Write the missing form of each verb.

	Singular	Plural
1.	plays	_____
2.	_____	guess
3.	_____	cough
4.	wishes	_____
5.	growls	_____
6.	_____	drive
7.	displays	_____
8.	thinks	_____
9.	_____	wax
10.	_____	dance

Directions: Write "S" for singular or "P" for plural on the blanks. Underline the verbs.

11. _____ People with phobatrivaphobia fear trivia about phobias.

12. _____ No matter how hard you try, you cannot lick your elbow.

13. _____ Male lions sleep up to 20 hours per day.

14. _____ American sculptor Alexander Calder rigged the front door of his Paris apartment so he could open it from the bathtub.

15. _____ A cockroach runs one meter per second.

16. _____ For a short distance, a hippopotamus can run faster than a person.

17. _____ Many students suffer from didaskaleinophobia.

18. _____ Didaskaleinophobia means the fear of going to school.

Name: _____ Date: _____

To Be, or Not to Be

A **verb** is a word that shows action or being. Verbs of being include: *feel, look, sound, taste, appear, grow, seem, smell,* and forms of *is.* Forms of *is* include *am, are, was, were, be,* and *been.*

Verbs of being are usually followed by a noun(s) or adjective(s) that shows a relationship.

Glenda is <u>happy</u>. (Adjective)

Glen was <u>lonely</u> and <u>scared</u>. (Adjectives)

Gwendolyn is a <u>girl</u>. (Noun)

Is your favorite pattern <u>plaid</u> or <u>polka-dots</u>? (Nouns)

Directions: Circle the verbs of being. Underline the two words that show a relationship. The first one has been done as an example.

1. <u>Pizza</u> (tastes) <u>great</u>.

2. Frankenstein felt hungry after he awoke.

3. He said, "Dinner smells delicious."

4. Did Spencer appear sad when you saw him after the movie?

5. A zebra is white with black stripes.

6. Did Grandpa feel sleepy after dinner?

7. They were elated at the good news.

8. My sister grew four inches taller last year.

9. You seem worried about something.

10. Hippopotomonstrosesquippedaliophobia is the fear of long words.

Directions: Write two sentences that use verbs of being about your favorite short story. Then circle the verbs of being and underline the two words that show a relationship.

_____

_____

_____

_____

_____

_____

_____

Name: _____ Date: _____

Past, Present, or Future?

Verbs use tense to show the time of the action.

• **Present tense** describes what is happening now.

He <u>is using</u> his new computer.

He <u>uses</u> his computer daily.

• **Past tense** describes what has already happened.

She <u>bought</u> a new computer program last week.

• **Future tense** describes what will happen.

We <u>will buy</u> a new computer in July.

Directions: Circle the verbs. Write "PR" for present, "PA" for past, or "F" for future.

1. _____ Joel washed his St. Bernard in the bathtub.

2. _____ Joel named his dog Minnie.

3. _____ Joel takes Minnie to obedience school every Tuesday.

4. _____ Minnie will learn to fetch large objects.

5. _____ Joel loves Minnie.

6. _____ The bears at the Cincinnati Zoo hibernated last winter.

7. _____ Did the bears at the San Diego Zoo hibernate?

8. _____ Will the groundhog see its shadow on February second?

9. _____ Can you come to the cottage next weekend?

10. _____ No one came to Sara's party last Saturday.

Directions: Write a verb in the tense indicated to finish the sentence.

11. Future tense: One of the major league teams

_____ Geoff.

12. Past tense: Who _____ first base for the Brewers last year?

13. Present tense: Tina _____ five miles every day.

Name: _____ Date: _____

Three Forms of Verbs

Verbs have three main forms: **present**, **past**, and **past participle**.

Use *had* with the past tense of a verb to form the **past perfect tense** of the **past participle** of regular verbs. Ad *-d* or *-ed* to form the past tense of most verbs.

They <u>had played</u> all day at the beach.

For one-syllable words ending in a single consonant preceded by a vowel, double the final consonant before adding *-ed*. For words ending in *y* after a consonant, change the *y* to *i* and add *-ed*.

For example:

Present	Past	Past Participle
hug	hugged	had hugged
skip	skipped	had skipped
party	partied	had partied

Directions: Write the missing verb forms for these regular verbs. Use a dictionary if you need help.

Present	Past	Past Participle
1. sail	_____	_____
2. mop	_____	_____
3. empty	_____	_____
4. jump	_____	_____
5. try	_____	_____
6. believe	_____	_____
7. sip	_____	_____
8. fry	_____	_____
9. push	_____	_____
10. imply	_____	_____

Name: _____ Date: _____

Sing, Sang, Sung

The **past** and **past participle** forms of most verbs are formed by adding -*d* or -*ed*. Verbs that do not follow this rule are called **irregular verbs**.

Present	Past	Past Participle
bring	brought	had brought
buy	bought	had bought
go	went	had gone
do	did	had done
fly	flew	had flown
grow	grew	had grown
ride	rode	had ridden
see	saw	had seen
sing	sang	had sung
swim	swam	had swum
throw	threw	had thrown

Do not use the past tense form of an irregular verb with the word *had*.

Correct: He <u>had flown</u> the plane to Florida.
Incorrect: He <u>had flew</u> the plane to Florida.

The word *had* can be separated from the verb by other words in the sentence.

<u>Had</u> you <u>seen</u> my blue sweater?

Directions: Using the irregular verb chart above, complete the sentences by writing the correct form of the verb shown in parentheses.

1. Had you ever _____ a camel? (ride)

2. Coach replaced the quarterback because he had _____ too many interceptions. (throw)

3. I can't believe he _____ that pass! (catch)

4. Her fig tree had _____ three inches taller while she was on vacation. (grow)

5. Where do you _____ when you want peace and quiet? (go)

6. Jerrod _____ to Phoenix for the winter. (go)

7. Had you ever _____ a sight like that? (see)

8. Cal _____ a jar of peanuts at the store. (buy)

Name: _____   Date: _____

At the White House

A **sentence** is a group of words that expresses a complete thought.

The White House did not have indoor plumbing until 1902.

- An incomplete sentence is called a **fragment**.

The Blue Room at the White House where the first lady.

- Every sentence needs a **subject** and a **predicate**. In some sentences, the subject is "you," and it is understood but not stated.

Please close the door. Help!

- A **simple sentence** has one subject and one predicate. A **compound sentence** has two or more subjects and/or predicates.

Directions: Read each group of words. If it expresses a complete thought, write "yes" on the blank. If not, write "no."

1. George Washington never lived in the White House.

   _____

2. A contest for the best design. _____

3. A fire in 1814 during the War of 1812. _____

4. During renovations to the White House between 1938 and 1952, the number of rooms increased from 62 to 132. _____

5. In spite of the many changes that have taken place, the White House and home of the President and his family.

   _____

6. Write a sentence with two subjects and one predicate.

   _____

   _____

   _____

7. Write a sentence with one subject and two predicates.

   _____

   _____

   _____

8. Write a sentence with two or more subjects and predicates.

   _____

   _____

   _____

   _____

Name: _____ Date: _____

What's the Question?

Capitalize the first word of a sentence. All sentences end with a period, question mark, or exclamation point.

- A sentence that asks a question ends with a **question mark**.

Would you hand me that mountain?

- A sentence that shows strong emotion ends with an **exclamation point**.

That's a great idea!

Directions: Write a complete sentence that shows strong emotion for each situation.

1. You won a terrific prize in the contest.

    _____

    _____

2. Todd found his missing pet snake.

    _____

    _____

3. Todd's mother found his missing pet snake.

    _____

    _____

4. Your neighbor had an unexpected visitor.

    _____

    _____

Directions: For each answer, write a short question.

5. _____ hot dogs

6. _____ bats

7. _____ 10 points

8. _____ yesterday

9. _____ 12 miles

10. _____ at the zoo

11. _____ Tom

12. _____ carefully

Name: _____   Date: _____

Please Hand Me That Mountain

A sentence that states a fact or gives a command ends in a **period**.

The walrus frowned at the iceberg.

Please hand me that mountain.

Directions: Write a short sentence to answer each question.

1. Where did they find it?

   _____

   _____

2. Why was she so grumpy?

   _____

   _____

3. How did you know the answer?

   _____

4. When did he lose it?

   _____

5. What did you see under the bed?

   _____

Directions: Write three sentences that are commands, but not questions.

6. _____

7. _____

8. _____

Directions: Add punctuation at the end of each sentence.

9. Why did the turkey cross the road

10. It was the chicken's day off

11. That's hilarious

12. Tell me another one, please

Name: _____ Date: _____

Rachel Giggled

The **simple predicate** of a sentence tells what the subject does, is doing, did, or will do. The simple predicate is always a **verb**.

The cat <u>sneezed</u>. (physical action)

Josh <u>thought</u> about the joke. (mental action)

Althea <u>is</u> sick. (state of being)

A sentence may have two or more predicates.

Althea <u>coughed</u>, <u>sneezed</u>, and <u>blew</u> her nose.

Directions: Circle the simple predicates. Write "A" if the verb is active, or "B" if the verb describes a state of being.

1. _____ The hungry dog ate the violin.

2. _____ Carlos danced in the forest.

3. _____ Would you please pass the sour milk?

4. _____ Eight green-eyed aliens arrived yesterday.

5. _____ Mustard is better with hot dogs than peanut butter or jelly.

6. _____ Tina baked and ate a jelly bean pizza.

7. _____ Jake traveled by submarine, and Angie rode in a hot-air balloon from California to New York.

8. _____ We are thrilled about our latest invention of breathable water.

9. _____ Macaroni is not a good material for building a house.

10. _____ Glass houses have brick fireplaces, but brick houses do not have glass fireplaces.

Directions: Write predicates to finish the sentences.

11. Felipe _____ the hot chili peppers.

12. I _____, he _____, and she _____ when we watched the strange movie.

Name: _____ Date: _____

Hey, Diddle, Diddle

The **simple subject** of a sentence is a noun or pronoun that is doing something or being something.

Subjects can be singular or plural.

<u>Miss Muffet</u> and three <u>spiders</u> ate lunch together.

More than one noun or pronoun can be the subject of a sentence.

Mary's little <u>lamb</u>, Bo Peep's <u>sheep</u>, and my little red <u>hen</u> searched for the treasure.

Directions: Circle the simple subjects. Remember, only nouns or pronouns can be the subjects, but not all nouns or pronouns in a sentence *are* subjects.

1. The big, bad wolf blew down the house made of sticks.

2. Can you and Little Boy Blue help Bo Peep find her sheep?

3. Jack jumped over the candlestick.

4. Can a cow jump over the moon?

5. The dish ran away with the spoon.

6. Did the mouse run up the clock?

7. Jack and Jill ran up the hill.

8. How do oats, peas, beans, and barley grow?

9. Jack jumped over the candlestick, and Mary chased her little lamb.

10. Old King Cole, his three fiddlers, the Knave of Hearts, and three blind mice went to the fair.

Directions: Write nouns or pronouns in the blanks to finish the sentences.

11. _____, _____, and _____ rode the rhinoceros.

12. _____ found a penny, and _____ picked it up.

13. _____ and _____ danced around the mulberry bush.

14. What did _____ find at the end of the rainbow?

Name: _____ Date: _____

Match-Ups

The subjects and predicates of a sentence **must agree in number**. If the subject is singular, then the predicate is singular.

<u>Marnie</u> <u>sings</u> like a canary.

<u>She</u> <u>is</u> a good singer.

If the subject is plural, then the predicate is plural. Use a plural verb in a sentence that has two or more singular subjects.

<u>Daniel and Danielle</u> <u>sing</u> well together.

<u>They</u> <u>are</u> twins.

Directions: Underline the subjects. Write "S" for singular or "P" for plural. Then write active verbs to finish the sentences.

1. _____ Lizards and snakes _____ in Florida.

2. _____ Everyone _____ bagpipe music.

3. _____ Chili with hot peppers _____ great.

4. _____ A squirrel, a snail, and a skunk _____ to the picnic.

5. _____ If a pig could _____, we would cheer.

6. _____ Does money _____ on trees on Venus?

7. _____ Does anyone still _____ that the earth is flat?

8. _____ The village _____ deep in the forest.

Directions: Write "S" for singular or "P" for plural to describe the verb. Then write nouns to finish the sentences.

9. _____ _____ fly.

10. _____ _____ dances.

11. _____ _____ bakes pumpkin bread.

12. _____ _____ eat sunflower seeds.

13. _____ _____ goes to the moon.

14. _____ _____ is tired.

Name: _____ Date: _____

Putting It All Together

A. Select five numbers between 1 and 26. Write them on the blanks in the "Numbers" column.

B. Select five letters between A and Z. Write them on the blanks in the "Letters" column.

C. Using the list on the next page, write the subjects and predicates that match the numbers and letters you wrote.

D. For each pair of words, write a complete sentence using a form of the two words you wrote as the subject and predicate, along with at least four other words.

Numbers	**Subjects**	**Letters**	**Predicates**
1. _____	_____	_____	_____
2. _____	_____	_____	_____
3. _____	_____	_____	_____
4. _____	_____	_____	_____
5. _____	_____	_____	_____

Name: _____ Date: _____

Putting It All Together (cont.)

Subjects		Predicates	
1.	aardvarks	A.	ate
2.	apples	B.	carried
3.	beans	C.	danced
4.	boat	D.	drove
5.	bus	E.	flew
6.	children	F.	gave
7.	dimples	G.	heard
8.	drums	H.	jumped
9.	farmer	I.	kicks
10.	goats	J.	looked
11.	judges	K.	marched
12.	jungle	L.	ran
13.	lawyers	M.	relaxed
14.	lizards	N.	said
15.	magicians	O.	sang
16.	music	P.	seemed
17.	mysteries	Q.	shouted
18.	people	R.	skated
19.	pigs	S.	smelled
20.	pizza	T.	stung
21.	sharks	U.	tasted
22.	shoes	V.	thought
23.	spiders	W.	threw
24.	squid	X.	wandered
25.	toys	Y.	wondered
26.	tubas	Z.	wrestled

Name: _____   Date: _____

Getting Personal

Pronouns take the place of nouns. They refer to people, places, things, or ideas.

The **antecedent** is the word replaced by a pronoun. If the antecedent is singular, use a singular pronoun. If the antecedent is plural, use a plural pronoun to replace it.

These pronouns can be used as subjects of sentences:

Singular	Plural
I	we
you	you
she, he, it	they

Directions: Write pronouns to replace the words in parentheses.

1. (The dragon) _____ breathed fire.

2. (The knight) _____ threw a bucket of water.

3. (The dragon) _____ began to steam.

4. (The men and women) _____ shouted, "Hurray!"

5. (The girl) _____ watched the knight ride his black horse into the sunset.

6. (Jamie and I) _____ want to be knights someday.

Directions: Write nouns to replace the underlined pronouns.

7. <u>We</u> _____ made friends with aliens from a distant galaxy.

8. <u>They</u> _____ traveled to Earth through time and space in a unique spaceship.

9. <u>It</u> _____ used carrot juice for fuel.

10. <u>He</u> _____ invited the aliens to visit the White House.

11. <u>She</u> _____ prepared 10,000 gallons of fresh carrot juice.

12. When the ship was refueled, <u>they</u> _____ took us to their planet.

Name: _____ Date: _____

They're Bringing Their Tubas

> **Possessive pronouns** show ownership.
>
> Possessive pronouns are:
>
> **Singular**
> my, mine
> your, yours
> her, hers, his, its
>
> **Plural**
> our, ours
> your, yours
> their, theirs
>
> Possessive pronouns must agree with their antecedents in number (singular or plural) and gender (male, female, or neuter).
>
> The dog went into <u>its</u> house.
>
> The children lost <u>their</u> way in the forest.

Directions: Fill in the blanks with possessive pronouns.

1. Marcy's trumpet is _____ trumpet.
   That trumpet is _____.

2. The tuba I play in the band is _____ tuba.
   That tuba is _____.

3. Jamal's bass drum is _____ drum.
   That bass drum is _____.

4. A treasure that belongs to you and me is _____ treasure.
   That treasure is _____.

5. Ted and Mei's song is _____ song.
   That song is _____.

6. The story you wrote last week is _____ story.
   That story is _____.

7. A hippo's loose tooth is _____ tooth.

8. The home where you and your family live is _____ home.
   That home is _____.

Name: _____ Date: _____

Don't Be Confused

Contractions are two words combined. An apostrophe shows that letters are missing.

Some contractions are often confused with possessive pronouns.

Contractions
you're = you are
it's = it is
they're = they are
there's = there is

Possessive Pronouns
your = belonging to you
its = belonging to it
their = belonging to them
theirs = belonging to them

Directions: Circle the correct words.

1. "(You're, Your) late," our coach complained.

2. "Put on (you're, your) uniform quickly," he continued.

3. "The rest of the team already put on (there's, theirs)."

4. "(There's, Theirs) no time to waste."

5. "(It's, Its) (you're, your) turn to bring the equipment."

6. "(They're, Their) ready to begin."

7. "The horseshoes are in (they're, their) cases."

8. "The stopwatch is in (it's, its) case on my desk."

Directions: Write a sentence using the pronoun or contraction listed.

9. they're _____

_____

_____

10. its _____

_____

_____

11. your _____

_____

_____

12. theirs _____

_____

_____

Name: _____ Date: _____

The Audience Threw Flowers

A **direct object** is a noun or pronoun. It answers the question *who* or *what* after the verb.

Mom bakes <u>bread</u>.

Bread is the direct object. It tells *what* Mom baked.

Mr. Clark hired <u>Randy</u> and <u>Lynn</u> to rake leaves.

Randy and *Lynn* are both direct objects. They tell *who* Mr. Clark hired.

An **indirect object** is a noun or pronoun. It answers the question *to whom* or *for whom* the action is performed. An indirect object is usually found between a verb and a direct object.

I gave <u>Elias</u> my e-mail address.

Elias is the indirect object. It tells *to whom* I gave my e-mail address.

Directions: Underline the direct objects.

1. Carla brought pizza, cake, and ice cream for the party.

2. Benji decorated the room and hung streamers in the windows.

3. Randy and Lynn raked leaves for Mr. Clark.

4. After Tasha sang the last song, the audience threw flowers.

5. Did Mia ride her bike or her motorcycle to school today?

Directions: Circle the indirect objects. Underline the direct objects.

6. Who gave Pedro that awful haircut?

7. Ellen sent Todd and Tami a wedding gift.

8. Mr. Clark gave Randy and Lynn $20.00 for their work.

9. Grandpa told Andy and Tori a story.

10. Uncle Joel showed Heather a magic trick.

11. Kimiko sang the baby a lullaby.

12. Did you give Devin the book?

Name: _____   Date: _____

What Fell From the Sky?

Who, *what*, and *which* are **interrogative pronouns**.

Use *who* when speaking of a person or persons.

> <u>Who</u> wore the cowboy hat?   The man <u>who</u> wore the cowboy hat was tall.

Use *what* when speaking of things.

> <u>What</u> fell from the sky?   No one knew <u>what</u> had fallen from the sky.

Use *which* when speaking of persons or things.

> <u>Which</u> woman wore the white woolen gown?
> <u>Which</u> do you like better: jugglers or clowns?

Who changes to *whom* when it is a direct object or an object of a preposition.

> To <u>whom</u> did you send the e-mail?

The possessive form of whom is *whose*.

> <u>Whose</u> e-mail address did you use?

Directions: Write *who*, *whom*, *whose*, *which*, or *what* in the blanks.

1. _____ movie won the most awards?

2. _____ played the leading role?

3. _____ fault was it that no one arrived on time?

4. Ask not for _____ the bell tolls.

5. The scientists found the answer for _____ they had been searching.

6. To _____ do we owe the honor of your presence?

7. _____ idea do you like best: Maria's or Joel's?

8. To _____ should we send the money order?

Name: _____ Date: _____

Stinky Cheese on Crisp, Crunchy Crackers

An **adjective** is a word that describes a noun or pronoun.

Smelly, silly, and *short* are adjectives.

Separate three or more adjectives in a row with a comma whether or not the word *and* is used.

Marty put the <u>large, frozen, mushroom</u> pizza in the oven.

Brett had three slices of the <u>hot, fresh, and delicious</u> homemade bread.

Directions: Write three or more adjectives to describe each noun. The first one has been done as an example.

1. *stinky, crumbly, Limburger* _____ cheese

2. _____ music

3. _____ software

4. _____ park

5. _____ library

6. _____ texture

7. _____ pineapple

8. _____ judge

9. _____ carpet

10. _____ weather

11. _____ jungle

12. _____ movie

Name: _____ Date: _____

Faster Than a Locomotive

Adjectives have three forms: **positive, comparative,** and **superlative**.

- The **positive** form is the adjective itself.

  Rosa thinks daisies are <u>pretty</u>.

- Use the **comparative** form to compare two people, places, things, or ideas.

  Rosa thinks daisies are <u>prettier</u> than violets.

- Use the **superlative** form when comparing three or more items.

  Daisy thinks roses are the <u>prettiest</u> flowers of all.

Guidelines:

Add -er at the end of most one-syllable adjectives to form the **comparative**.

For two-syllable words ending in y, change the y to i and add -er.

For short words ending in e, simply add r.

For short words with the consonant/vowel/consonant (CVC) pattern, double the final consonant before adding -er.

When in doubt, check a dictionary.

Directions: Write the comparative or superlative form of an adjective in each sentence.

1. Is Flora _____ than Violet?

2. What is the _____ mountain on Mars?

3. Which river is _____, the Amazon or the Nile?

4. Where is the _____ canyon in North America?

5. Have you ever seen falls _____ than Niagara Falls?

6. The _____ day on record was at the South Pole.

7. It rarely gets _____ than 85 degrees in Hawaii.

8. For each pair, the winner is the one who runs _____.

9. The tortoise was _____ than the hare, but he won the race.

10. Of all mammals, which runs the _____?

Name: _____　Date: _____

Long, Longer, Longest, But Never Wrong, Wronger, Wrongest

Combine the adjective with the word *more* or *most* to form the **comparative** and **superlative** form of most two-syllable words that do not end in *y*.

Form the comparative and superlative form of all adjectives with three or more syllables by combining the adjective with the word *more* or *most*.

Positive	Comparative	Superlative
modern	more modern	most modern
beautiful	more beautiful	most beautiful

Some adjectives change completely to form the comparative and superlative, such as *good - better - best*.

Directions: Write the comparative and superlative forms of these adjectives.

	Positive	Comparative	Superlative
1.	floppy	_____	_____
2.	slow	_____	_____
3.	expensive	_____	_____
4.	happy	_____	_____
5.	late	_____	_____
6.	heavy	_____	_____

Directions: Write the comparative and superlative forms of these adjectives. Use a dictionary if you need help.

	Positive	Comparative	Superlative
7.	far	_____	_____
8.	bad	_____	_____
9.	many	_____	_____
10.	well (healthy)	_____	_____

Name: _____ Date: _____

Use Your Senses

Directions: For each sense, write three or more nouns, verbs, and adjectives in additon to the samples given. Use a dictionary or thesaurus if you need ideas.

Sight
Nouns: Eyes _____

Verbs: Look _____

Adjectives: Beautiful _____

Sound
Nouns: Ears _____

Verbs: Hear _____

Adjectives: Loud _____

Smell
Nouns: Snout _____

Verbs: Sniff _____

Adjectives: Delicious _____

Taste
Nouns: Tongue _____

Verbs: Nibble _____

Adjectives: Creamy _____

Feel
Nouns: Hands _____

Verbs: Caress _____

Adjectives: Silky _____

Name: _____   Date: _____

On the Way to Denver

An **adverb** is a word that modifies a verb, adjective, or another adverb by describing, limiting, or making the meaning of a word more clear.

Eric Carle wrote *The Very Hungry Caterpillar.*

The word *very* is an adverb that modifies the adjective *hungry.* It tells *how* hungry.

Adverbs answer the questions *why, where, when, how,* or *to what extent.*

Tomorrow, far, shortly, quickly, and *abruptly* are adverbs.

Directions: Circle the adverb in each sentence. Underline the word(s) it modifies. Write the question the adverb answers. The first one has been done as an example.

1. The truck driver <u>unloaded</u> the trailer (quickly)

   How did the driver unload the trailer? _____

2. She drove eagerly to the next truck stop.

   _____

3. After a short rest, she filled the gas tank completely.

   _____

4. She traveled far on the long, winding mountain road.

   _____

5. She will arrive in Denver tomorrow.

   _____

6. She played the radio quietly while she drove.

   _____

7. Too soon, it began to snow.

   _____

8. The snow-covered road eventually became very slippery.

   _____

   _____

Name: _____ Date: _____

Soon, Sooner, Soonest

Like adjectives, **adverbs** have three forms: **positive, comparative,** and **superlative**.

- The **positive** form is the adverb itself.

  Jason will be here <u>soon</u>.

- Use the **comparative** form to compare two events.

  Jason will arrive <u>sooner</u> than Grandpa.

- Use the **superlative** form when comparing three or more items.

  Of all the guests, Jason will arrive the <u>soonest</u>.

Guidelines:
- Add *-er* to the end of most one-syllable adverbs to form the **comparative**.
- Add *-est* to the end of most one-syllable adverbs to form the **superlative**.
- For most adverbs ending in *-ly*, combine the adverb with the word *more* or *less* for **comparative**, and *most* or *least* for **superlative**.

brightly	more brightly	most brightly
noisily	less noisily	least noisily

Some adverbs are irregular. When in doubt, check a dictionary.

Directions: Write the comparative or superlative form of an adjective in each sentence.

1. Is Chantal reading _____ than she did yesterday?

2. She acted the _____ of all the students.

3. Ask the children to play _____ than they did yesterday.

4. Dion takes life much _____ than his sister does.

5. This book is written _____ than the last one by the same author.

6. He unwrapped the second package _____ than he did the first one.

7. Mike did badly on the test, but Jeremy did even _____.

8. Which of the three statues do you think is _____ carved?

Name: _____ Date: _____

Adjective or Adverb?

Many **adjectives** can be changed to an adverb by adding *-ly* to the end of the word. If the word ends in *y*, change the *y* to *i*, and add *-ly*.

quiet   quietly
slow   slowly
hungry   hungrily
dainty   daintily

Use an **adjective** to describe a noun or pronoun. Use an **adverb** to modify a verb, adjective, or other adverb.

He made a <u>quick</u> trip to the store.

<u>Quick</u> is an adjective describing trip.

He ran <u>quickly</u> to the store.

<u>Quickly</u> is an adverb. It tells how he ran.

Directions: State whether the underlined word in each sentence is an adjective (ADJ) or an adverb (ADV) and why.

1. He has <u>strong</u> feelings for his brother. _____

   Why?_____

2. He felt <u>strongly</u> that his brother was wrong. _____

   Why?_____

3. I can tell when danger is <u>near</u>. _____

   Why?_____

4. Are we <u>nearly</u> there? _____

   Why?_____

5. Take me to the <u>nearest</u> ice cream stand. _____

   Why?_____

6. The trail is <u>longer</u> than I thought it would be. _____

   Why?_____

7. Joanne giggled <u>happily</u>. _____

   Why?_____

8. Tony's dog won <u>first</u> prize. _____

   Why?_____

9. Which came <u>first</u>: the chicken or the egg? _____

   Why?_____

10. Tomorrow is <u>another</u> day. _____

    Why?_____

Name: _____ Date: _____

Across the Wide Missouri

A **preposition** is a word that comes before a noun or pronoun and shows its relationship to some other word in the sentence.

Common Prepositions

about	down	off	through	above	for	on	to
across	from	out	up	at	in	over	with
behind	into	near	within	by	of	past	without

The **object of a preposition** is a noun or pronoun that follows a preposition and adds to its meaning. A preposition must be followed by a noun or pronoun.

A **prepositional phrase** includes the preposition, the object of the preposition, and all modifiers.

Gertrude Ederle was the first woman to swim across the English Channel.

<u>Across</u> is the preposition.
<u>Across the English Channel</u> is the prepositional phrase.
<u>English Channel</u> is the object of the preposition.

Directions: Complete the prepositional phrases. Underline the prepositions. Circle the nouns or pronouns that are objects of the prepositions.

1. _____ the flea circus

2. _____ the tallest tree

3. inside the empty _____

4. without any possible _____

5. past the _____ mountains

6. _____ the ice-covered rooftops

7. _____ the dark and gloomy forest

8. near the _____ ancient castle

9. _____ the south side of the _____

10. _____ the _____

Name: _____ Date: _____

When in Rome

A **preposition** is a word that comes before a noun or pronoun and shows its relationship to some other word in the sentence.

A **proverb** is a saying that most people accept as true and that implies a deeper meaning.

"When in Rome, do as the Romans do."

Directions: Underline the prepositions and enclose the prepositional phrases in parentheses. Circle the nouns or pronouns that are the objects of the prepositions. The first one has been done as an example. Some proverbs may contain more than one prepositional phrase.

1. Don't cry (<u>over</u> spilt (milk)).

2. A bird in the hand is worth two in the bush.

3. A journey of a thousand miles begins with a single step.

4. People in glass houses should not throw stones.

5. Never look a gift horse in the mouth.

6. The grass is always greener on the other side of the fence.

7. Rome wasn't built in a day.

8. Birds of a feather flock together.

9. Necessity is the mother of invention.

10. Great oaks from little acorns grow.

11. You can't make a silk purse from a sow's ear.

12. It's all water under the bridge.

Directions: Select one of the above proverbs and rewrite it in your own words. "Don't cry over spilt milk" could be rewritten as: "If you can't do something about a situation, move on."

_____

_____

_____

Name: _____ Date: _____

She Met Him and Me

Use **objective pronouns** as direct objects, indirect objects, or objects of a preposition.

Objective Pronouns

Singular: *me, you, him, her, it*
Plural: *us, you, them*

Two or more nouns or pronouns can be the direct objects of a sentence.

Aunt June met <u>him</u> and <u>me</u> at the bus station.

Dana liked <u>him</u> better than <u>her</u>.

Two or more nouns or pronouns can be the objects of a preposition.

Dave played the game with <u>her</u> and <u>him</u>.

Mom received gifts from <u>her</u> and <u>me</u>.

Directions: Fill in the blanks with objective pronouns. Write "DO" for direct object, "IO" for indirect object, or "OP" for object of a preposition within the parentheses to show how each pronoun is used.

1. Tina saw _____ and _____ at the pool.

   (_____)

2. Will you meet _____ at Pier 49?

   (_____)

3. The party was for _____ and _____.

   (_____)

4. The plumber gave _____ and _____ the

   bad news.   (_____)

5. Marsha received phone calls from _____ and

   _____.   (_____)

6. Mom gave _____ a pail, and Dad gave

   _____ a broom.   (_____)

7. Tiffany lent the book to _____, but Dave forgot

   to give it back to _____.   (_____)

8. Uncle Frank brought _____ and _____

   souvenirs from the North Pole.   (_____)

9. Did Buster drive _____ and _____ to San

   Francisco?   (_____)

10. Are you going to the amusement park with _____?

   (_____)

Name: _____ Date: _____

He Knew the New Gnu

Homophones are words that sound the same, but are spelled differently and have different meanings.

He <u>knew</u> the <u>new</u> <u>gnu</u> would be at the zoo today.

Directions: Circle the correct word in each pair. Write the part of speech of the word you circled on the line next to the sentence. Use a dictionary if you need help.

1. _____ Our ship (sails, sales) for
   _____ Cancun next (weak, week).

2. _____ I can't (wait, weight)
   _____ (to, two, too) leave.

3. _____ Jean bought her jeans on (sail,
   sale).

4. _____ She paid full price for the first
   _____ (pair, pear) and only 99 (sense,
   _____ cents) for the second one.

5. _____ Do you like (red, read) roses
   _____ or (blew, blue) carnations
   better?

6. _____ When the (brakes, breaks)
   failed, his car slid down the hill.

7. _____ Clark lost his (way, weigh)
   _____ when he (maid, made) a
   _____ (write, right) turn in a small town
   _____ in (Maine, Main).

8. _____ Don't (stair, stare) at the man
   _____ wearing the (fur, fir) shirt.

9. _____ Sandy looked (pail, pale)
   _____ because she had the (flu, flew).

10. _____ He (knew, new) that
    _____ (four, for, fore) plus
    _____ (to, two, too) equals
    _____ six, but he didn't (no, know)
    _____ that seven plus (won, one)
    _____ equals (ate, eight)?

Name: _____ Date: _____

What's the Connection?

Conjunctions are words that connect two or more words or groups of words. *And, but, or, nor, so,* and *because* are conjunctions.

Join two short sentences with the word *and* when the sentences are about equal.

Juan will arrive at noon, <u>and</u> he will be hungry.

Join two short sentences with the word *but* when the second sentence contradicts the first.

Juan will arrive at lunchtime, <u>but</u> he will not be hungry.

Join two short sentences with the word *or* when they name a choice.

Juan may be on time, <u>or</u> he may be late.

Join two short sentences with *because* or *so* when the second sentence names a reason for the first sentence.

Juan will be on time <u>because</u> he is very punctual.

Directions: Write conjunctions to complete the sentences.

1. Barry doesn't like prune juice, _____ he likes prunes.

2. Tori overslept, _____ she was late for school.

3. Would you like ham on your pizza, _____ would you rather have tuna?

4. The river overflowed _____ the dam broke.

Directions: Finish the sentences.

5. Marta will sing in the choir, or _____

6. Marta will sing in the choir because _____

7. Marta will sing in the choir, and _____

Name: _____ Date: _____

Did He Really Say That?

The principle parts of speech are **nouns, pronouns, verbs, adjectives, adverbs, prepositions,** and **conjunctions.**

Directions: Read these quotations from former baseball great Yogi Berra. Name the parts of speech for the underlined words.

1. _____ "<u>You</u> can't think and hit at the same time."

2. _____ "Nobody goes there, it's <u>too</u> crowded."

3. _____ "A nickel ain't worth a <u>dime</u> anymore."

4. _____ We were <u>overwhelming</u> underdogs."

5. _____ "The other team could make trouble for <u>us</u> if they win."

6. _____ "When you come to a fork in the road, <u>take</u> it."

7. _____ "It's never happened in World Series history, <u>and</u> it hasn't happened since."

8. _____ "I <u>usually</u> take a two-hour nap from 1 to 4."

9. _____ "We're lost, <u>but</u> we're making good time."

10. _____ "If I didn't wake <u>up</u>, I'd still be sleeping."

11. _____ "I wish I had an answer to that <u>because</u> I'm tired of answering that question."

12. _____ "It's not too far; it just seems like <u>it</u> is."

13. _____ "We <u>made</u> too many wrong mistakes."

14. _____ "You've got to be careful if <u>you</u> don't know where you're going 'cause you might not get there."

15. _____ "We have a good <u>time</u> together, even when we're not together."

Name: _____ Date: _____

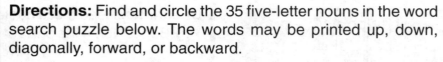

Five-Letter Nouns

A **noun** is the name of a person, place, thing, or idea. *Pumpkin, nose, starfish, kindness,* and *Chicago* are nouns.

Directions: Find and circle the 35 five-letter nouns in the word search puzzle below. The words may be printed up, down, diagonally, forward, or backward.

acorn	apple	apron	candy	canoe	flour
frown	goose	lemon	month	moose	motor
mouse	night	nurse	onion	paper	party
peace	peach	photo	piano	plant	radio
robin	robot	siren	stone	stork	stuff
title	tooth	uncle	video	wheel	

```
U L H N N E S R U N A B I J U O R O B O T G C L
K K K Z R U C H Z X D H Q O F F U T S P O B C D
D U P O O O N P X K N Q G O R L F J D O B O N Y
T L D M B G B E M A Y J N I U N P O S T D O R P
M E N L P K D I V B J W O D S B H E A N I M X E
F E Z O G R U L N F O N C A P R O K M N A R M A
O H K R U O L B P R W X J R T M T I O P J W Q C
D W T C X T Q E F O Q E P L Y I O M P U O D L E
A N E T P S O A F L V Z Y R W K Y L P N O M Z U
Y W P I Z X E W E Q E M V O T Q E F A C Z T T Q
R T A Q Y E D G I J O O L T Y L X E Z L O I D H
O N M T E T I Q O O Y M C O Q I U Y W E X E P Y
O F R Z N C V W S V L A Z M W T N A T G I L A A
M A K O Q R Y E T W N G P A U M P R V I V T N S
P G R E V F M T C D T X F D D Q L E J U C I H J
W P C P L V I P Y P L T Q V U P A P N S H T K I
A Q X O C O V I Q E O C Z T W F N A X I N Q S B
I E U B J M L T O O A P P X S M T P X T G I O F
W R Q H O Y U Y T H E I W S T L Y V C M R H D C
O D F U C G S H C D O L E M O N F R F E O W T I
U P S H S K G N T G N R D U N X N L N G R N B J
G E S L E Q W K I M A G K T E L R O Y M I N T R
T A C O R N D G B E C X A I B M P E A C H H M H
R Z U L U H Q F Y I B C V R F H I O F O C R T T
```

Name: _____   Date: _____

Mabel Likes to Polka in Her Polka-dotted Dress

Some words can be used **as more than one part of speech.**

Dance can be a noun, a verb, or an adjective.

Would you like to go to the <u>dance</u>? (noun)

Will you <u>dance</u> with me tomorrow? (verb)

The <u>dance</u> instructor taught me to waltz. (adjective)

Directions: Write short sentences using the words as the parts of speech indicated in parentheses. Use a dictionary if you need help. Use your own paper if you need more room.

1. dress (noun) _____

   _____

   dress (verb) _____

   _____

   dress (adjective) _____

   _____

2. guard (noun) _____

   guard (verb) _____

   guard (adjective) _____

3. light (noun) _____

   light (verb) _____

   light (adjective) _____

4. brown (noun) _____

   brown (verb) _____

   brown (adjective) _____

5. mine (pronoun) _____

   mine (noun) _____

   mine (verb) _____

Name: _____ Date: _____

Parts of Speech Bingo Card

Directions to the Teacher: Give each student a copy of a blank Parts of Speech Bingo card and game markers. Have students write the name of one of these parts of speech in each square: noun, pronoun, adjective, adverb, verb, or preposition.

Make a copy of the word list on the next two pages on a heavy paper or light cardboard. Cut the words apart and place them in a bag. Draw one word at a time. Read the word to the class, using it in a sentence, and then write the part of speech on the slip of paper with the word. Students should cover the square on their Bingo card that matches that part of speech. Play like regular Bingo. Have students write the word in the square, so you can check if the correct part of speech has been chosen.

		Free		

Parts of Speech Bingo Word List

about	cake	empty	frozen	hog
air	calmly	entire	fully	honest
alertly	candy	equal	funny	honesty
almost	carry	equally	furry	hop
always	cattle	eternal	fuzzy	humid
among	city	evenly	gentle	I
around	cleanly	exact	gently	ideal
at	clearly	exactly	give	ideally
ate	closely	exotic	gladly	ideas
badly	coat	extreme	glassy	in
banker	coldly	famous	gloomy	instant
barely	coolly	fancy	goat	it
barn	country	farmer	golden	itchy
beans	crisply	fearful	grand	its
beauty	daily	feel	grandly	jolly
before	darkly	final	greedy	joy
behind	day	flatly	grimy	judge
between	dearly	fleet	grumpy	juicy
big	deeply	flower	gusty	jump
bitter	desert	fluffy	hairy	jumpy
black	dimly	flutes	happily	jungle
bleak	dimples	foggy	happy	kind
boat	direct	fondly	hastily	kindly
bond	dirty	forest	he	largely
bored	distant	forever	healthy	largest
brave	dizzy	former	hear	lately
bravely	drably	forward	heavily	lazily
breezy	drowsy	fragile	heavy	leafy
bright	drums	frantic	helpful	level
brisk	dusty	freely	hers	lightly
briskly	eager	fresh	hidden	little
broken	eagerly	freshly	highly	lizard
bumpy	early	frisky	hilly	lonely
bus	easily	from	him	loudly
butter	elegant	frosty	his	love

Parts of Speech Bingo Word List (cont.)

lovely	over	regal	tender	violin
luckily	oxen	relax	their	visit
lucky	pail	remote	theirs	waddle
lumpy	painted	restless	them	warmly
mainly	patient	richly	they	we
marshy	peace	roaring	thick	wealthy
mellow	perfect	rocky	thorny	weary
mildly	pizza	rough	through	weld
mine	plaid	roughly	throw	well
misty	plain	round	tight	whisker
month	plainly	rudely	timely	widely
moody	poetic	run	timid	willing
moon	poorly	sadly	tiny	wince
mostly	popular	said	tired	windy
moth	pretty	sang	to	wing
music	proper	see	total	wisely
musical	proud	she	toward	witty
my	puzzled	shoe	toy	wood
mystery	quaint	shouted	truly	worthy
narrow	quick	shyly	twisted	yam
natural	quickly	sing	under	yard
nearly	quiet	skip	uneasy	yearly
neatly	quietly	sleep	uneven	yelp
needy	quill	slowly	unhappy	yield
nervous	radish	smell	unique	yodel
never	ragged	snake	unknown	yogurt
newly	rainy	softly	unusual	you
nicely	rake	soon	us	yours
night	rapid	squid	usually	zany
normal	rapidly	sun	vacant	zap
often	rarely	tactful	valley	zeal
on	reach	take	vastly	zealously
once	read	tamely	velvet	zenith
our	really	tangled	very	zesty
ours	recent	taste	vex	zipped

Answer Keys

From Aardvarks to Zippers (p. 2)
1. ball; dimples
2. sharks; fish; eyes
3. 1927; service; New York; London; $75.00; minutes
4. telephones; 1899
5. yo-yo; invention; children; Rome; toys; wood; metal; years

Leaves, Potatoes, and Daisies (p. 3)
1. leaves
2. flies
3. trophies
4. elves
5. hippopotamuses or hippopotami
6. skies
7. buses or busses
8. oxen
9. addresses
10. boxes

11–20. Answers will vary. Possible answers are listed.
11. land
12. answers
13. children
14. enemies
15. nights
16. floors
17. uncle
18. freedom
19. country
20. frown

Do Mouses Live in Houses? (p. 4)
1. men
2. women
3. geese
4. lice
5. scissors
6. sheep
7. moose
8. teeth
9. feet
10. fish or fishes
11. deer
12. data
13. crises
14. bacteria
15. analyses

London Bridge Is Not in England Anymore (p. 5)
1. George Washington; Thomas Jefferson; Abraham Lincoln; Theodore Roosevelt; Mount Rushmore; Black Hills; South Dakota; Gutzon Borglum
2. Yellowstone National Park; Wyoming; Montana; Idaho; President Ulysses S. Grant
3. Maine; Maryland; Massachusetts; Michigan; Minnesota; Mississippi; Missouri; Montana
4. Harriet Tubman; Moses; Underground Railroad
5. Thanksgiving; Thursday; November

6–9. Answers will vary.

Hop, Skip, and Jump (p. 6)
Answers will vary.

Strange, But True (p. 7)
1. play
2. guesses
3. coughs
4. wish
5. growl
6. drives
7. display
8. think
9. waxes
10. dances
11. P, fear
12. P, try; lick
13. P, sleep
14. S, rigged; could open
15. S, runs
16. S, can run
17. P, suffer
18. S, means

To Be, or Not to Be (p. 8)
1. Pizza (tastes) great
2. Frankenstein (felt) hungry
3. Dinner (smells) delicious
4. Spencer (Did appear) sad
5. zebra (is) white
6. Grandpa (Did feel) sleepy
7. They (were) elated
8. sister (grew) taller
9. You (seem) worried
10. Hippopotomonstrosesquippedaliophobia (is) fear

Past, Present, or Future? (p. 9)
1. PA; washed   2. PA; named
3. PR; takes   4. F; will learn
5. PR; loves   6. PA; hibernated
7. PA; did hibernate   8. F; will see
9. F; can come   10. PA; came
11–13. Answers will vary.

Three Forms of Verbs (p. 10)
1. sailed; had sailed
2. mopped; had mopped
3. emptied;had emptied
4. jumped; had jumped
5. tried; had tried
6. believed; had believed
7. sipped; had sipped
8. fried; had fried
9. pushed; had pushed
10. implied; had implied

Sing, Sang, Sung (p. 11)
1. ridden   2. thrown
3. caught   4. grown
5. go   6. went
7. seen   8. bought

At the White House (p. 12)
1. yes   2. no   3. no
4. yes   5. no
6–8. Answers will vary.

What's the Question? (p. 13)
Answers will vary.

Please Hand Me That Mountain (p. 14)
1–8. Answers will vary.
9. question mark   10. period
11. exclamation point   12. period

Rachel Giggled (p. 15)
1. A; ate   2. A; danced
3. A; would pass   4. A; arrived

5. B; is
6. A; A; baked; ate
7. A; A; traveled; rode
8. B; are
9. B; is
10. B; B; have; do have
11–12. Answers will vary.

Hey, Diddle, Diddle (p. 16)
1. wolf   2. you; Little Boy Blue
3. Jack   4. cow
5. dish   6. mouse
7. Jack; Jill
8. oats; peas; beans; barley
9. Jack; Mary
10. Old King Cole; fiddlers; Knave; mice
11–14. Answers will vary.

Match-Ups (p. 17)
Verbs will vary.
1. P; lizards, snakes
2. S; Everyone
3. S; Chili
4. P; squirrel, snail, skunk
5. S; pig
6. S; money
7. S; anyone
8. S; village
Nouns will vary.
9. P   10. S   11. S   12. P
13. S   14. S

Putting It All Together (p. 18)
Answers will vary.

Getting Personal (p. 20)
1. It   2. He   3. It
4. They   5. She   6. We
7-12. Answers will vary.

They're Bringing Their Tubas (p. 21)
1. her; hers	2. my; mine
3. his; his	4. our; ours
5. their; theirs	6. your; yours
7. its	8. your; yours

Don't Be Confused (p. 22)
1. You're	2. your
3. theirs	4. There's
5. It's, your	6. They're
7. their	8. its

9–12. Answers will vary.

The Audience Threw Flowers (p. 23)
1. pizza, cake, ice cream
2. room, streamers
3. leaves
4. song, flowers
5. bike, motorcycle
6. Pedro   haircut
7. Todd, Tami   gift
8. Randy, Lynn $20.00
9. Andy, Tori   story
10. Heather   trick
11. baby   lullaby
12. Devin   book

What Fell From the Sky? (p. 24)
1. Which or What	2. Who
3. Whose	4. whom
5. which	6. what
7. Whose or Which or What	
8. whom	

Stinky Cheese on Crisp, Crunchy, Crackers (p. 25)
Answers will vary.

Faster Than a Locomotive (p. 26)
Answers will vary. Please be certain that students use the comparative or superlative form as indicated.

1. comparative	2. superlative
3. comparative	4. superlative
5. comparative	6. superlative
7. comparative	8. comparative
9. comparative	10. superlative

Long, Longer, Longest, But Never Wrong, Wronger, Wrongest (p. 27)
1. floppier; floppiest
2. slower; slowest
3. more expensive; most expensive
4. happier; happiest
5. later; latest
6. heavier; heaviest
7. farther; farthest
8. worse; worst
9. more; most
10. better; best

Use Your Senses (p. 28)
Answers will vary.

On the Way to Denver (p. 29)
1. quickly   unloaded
2. eagerly   drove
3. completely   filled
4. far   traveled
5. tomorrow   will arrive
6. quietly   played
7. Too   soon;   soon   began
8. eventually   became;   very   slippery

Soon, Sooner, Soonest (p. 30)
Answers will vary.

1. comparative	2. superlative
3. comparative	4. comparative
5. comparative	6. comparative
7. comparative	8. superlative

Adjective or Adverb? (p. 31)

1.	ADJ	2.	ADV
3.	ADJ	4.	ADV
5.	ADJ	6.	ADJ
7.	ADV	8.	ADJ
9.	ADV	10.	ADJ

Across the Wide Missouri (p. 32)

Answers will vary.

When in Rome (p. 33)

1. (<u>over</u> spilt (milk))
2. (<u>in</u> the (hand)) (<u>in</u> the (bush))
3. (<u>of</u> a thousand (miles)) (<u>with</u> a single (step))
4. (<u>in</u> glass (houses))
5. (<u>in</u> the (mouth))
6. (<u>on</u> the other (side)) (<u>of</u> the (fence))
7. (<u>in</u> a (day))
8. (<u>of</u> a (feather))
9. (<u>of</u> (invention))
10. (<u>from</u> little (acorns))
11. (<u>from</u> a sow's (ear))
12. (<u>under</u> the (bridge))

She Met Him and Me (p. 34)

1.	DO	2.	DO	3.	OP
4.	IO	5.	OP	6.	IO; IO
7.	OP; OP	8.	IO	9.	DO
10.	OP				

He Knew the New Gnu (p. 35)

1. sails (verb); week (noun)
2. wait (verb); to (preposition)
3. sale (noun)
4. pair (noun); cents (noun)
5. red (adjective); blue (adjective)
6. brakes (noun)
7. way (noun); made (verb); right (adjective); Maine (noun)
8. stare (verb); fur (adjective)

9. pale (adjective); flu (noun)
10. knew (verb); four (noun); two (noun); know (verb); one (noun); eight (noun)

What's the Connection? (p. 36)

1. but   2. and/so   3. or
4. because
5–7. Answers will vary.

Did He Really Say That? (p. 37)

1.	pronoun	2.	adverb
3.	noun	4.	adjective
5.	pronoun	6.	verb
7.	conjunction	8.	adverb
9.	conjunction	10.	adverb
11.	conjunction	12.	pronoun
13.	verb	14.	pronoun
15.	noun		

Five-Letter Nouns (p. 38)

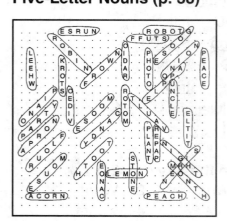

Mabel Likes to Polka in Her Polka-dotted Dress (p. 39)

Answers will vary.